After the Affair

Emotional Healing God's Way for Church and Ministry Leaders

Also by Arnita Lafaye Fields

After the Affair, Emotional Healing God's Way
Prayer Journal (After the Affair Book Series-Book #2)

After the Affair, Emotional Healing God's Way
(After the Affair Book Series-Book #1)

Drop That Bottle and Pick up a Fork!
Poetry, Prophetic Revelation and the Word of God

Covenant Sisterhood
Embracing Heaven's Divine Connections

Keeping the Faith Anthology (Co-Author)

America's Change, a Poetic View

THE WORD a Poetry Connection

This Far By Faith Anthology (Co-Author)

And the Beat Goes On
Poems from a Restored Marriage

Rescued, Restored, Renewed & Revived
A Collection of Christian Poems

I'll Be Home for Christmas Anthology (Co-Author)

After the Affair

*Emotional Healing God's Way
for Church and Ministry Leaders*

Arnita Lafaye Fields

Unity Three Publications
Memphis, Tennessee

After the Affair: Emotional Healing God's Way for Church and Ministry Leaders

ISBN: 978-0-578-14968-4

First Printing

www.aftertheaffairemotionalhealinggodsway.blogspot.com

Editor: Shelia E. Bell, Written Word Editorial Services
writtenwordeditorial@gmail.com

Library of Congress Control Number: 2014915608

Book Cover Design: Kool Design Maker
www.kooldesignmaker.com

Printed in the United States of America

Dedication

For church and ministry leaders everywhere who have secretly struggled with any form of sexual sin while serving God.

Acknowledgements

Heavenly Father, I give you praise for your continued direction, provision, and protection. Every day of my journey with you, I have been simply amazed by your love.

To my beloved husband, Anthony, thank you as always for your love, friendship, laughter, and faithful support.

To my parents, thank you for your prayers and continued support.

Table of Contents

Message from the Author

After the Affair: Emotional Healing God's Way for Church and Ministry Leaders is the third and final installment in the *After the Affair* book series. Its purpose is to serve as a source of information for church and ministry leaders who may need practical wisdom in assisting team members within their organizations who may now be dealing, or have dealt with, the negative effects of sexual sin.

No matter how deep a person has fallen into any sin, the Father has already provided a way of escape through Christ and the finished work of the cross.

May the information presented within these pages, along with prayer and the word of God, help guide you as a leader to not only understand the plight of those affected, but also offer insight on how to restore and release hope in the true love of the Father.

If additional assistance is needed, I have listed some resources at the end of the book for you to pass along.

Blessings

Arnita LaFaye Fields
Christian Counselor

Introduction

Over the course of the last few years, there has been a significant increase in the sexual sin issues of many church and ministry leaders played out in the public forum. While often orchestrated and facilitated by the media or other outside sources, the shortcomings of these marriages were highlighted. The fallen were immediately condemned and cast aside without ever receiving the proper care, healing, and restoration that they so desperately needed.

In an effort to address, and then offer practical solutions to help alleviate this ongoing issue, the information supplied within these pages will offer church and ministry leader's ways to assist those within their organizations who may need spiritual help gaining freedom from all forms of **sexual sin,** which is rooted in the stronghold of lust. By no means was this book written to judge those who have fallen to sexual sin or to give them a free pass. The goal, however, is to assist leaders and their teams on how to minister effectively as spiritual agents of reconciliation

The information in this book will cover five key areas, along with questions for discussion. The stronghold of lust, which serves as the root of all sexual sin will be discussed along with the subjects of adultery and pornography as two of the main areas of sexual sin which is prevalent not only in secular society but has been increasing at a rapid and alarming rate within many church and ministry settings.

1. Lust: the Root of all Sexual Sin
2. Dissecting Adultery
3. Print and Digital Pornography
4. When Leaders Fall
5. Confidentiality and Disclosure

Lust: the Root of all Sexual Sin

The stronghold of **lust** can be traced all the way back to Biblical times. In fact, it is first mentioned in Genesis 6 when Eve lusted for (desired) the fruit from the tree in the middle of the garden. Throughout the Bible, we find many stories where people were taken and overcome by the negative effects of lust.

I John 2:16 warns us, "For everything in the world, the lust of the flesh, the lust of the eyes, and the pride of life comes not from the Father but from the world."

When Jesus Christ the Son of God went to the cross, He died for every sin, including any addictive behavior. Because of His great sacrifice, there was not one area of the flesh that He did not touch.

In order for people who struggle with lust to maintain deliverance, it is important for them to not only accept and receive the deliverance that Jesus already provided for them on the cross, but to also counter and deal with the stronghold of lust so they can remain free.

Before we go into how a person can gain freedom from lust, first we will look at both the natural and spiritual definitions in order to have a clear understanding of how lust operates.

Merriam Webster Dictionary describes lust as:

1. A strong feeling of sexual desire
2. A strong desire *for* something
3. Pleasure, delight
4. Personal inclination: wish
5. Usually intense or unbridled sexual desire: lasciviousness
6. An intense longing: craving (a lust to succeed).

Eaton Bible Dictionary describes lust as follows:

A sinful longing and the inward sin which leads to the falling away from God (see Romans 1:21). Lust, the origin of sin, has its place in the heart, not of necessity, but because it is the centre of all moral forces and impulses and of spiritual activity. In Mark 4:19 "lusts" are objects of desire.

Following are several passages of scripture that reveal how the stronghold of lust begins and manifests into what may be desired by a person.

Genesis 3:6 "So when the woman saw that the tree was good for food, that it was pleasant to the eyes, and a tree desirable to make one wise, she took of its fruit and ate. She also gave to her husband with her, and he ate."

Exodus 20:17 "You shall not covet your neighbor's house; you shall not covet your neighbor's wife, nor his male servant, nor his female servant, nor his ox, nor his donkey, nor anything that is your neighbor's."

Psalm 81:12 "So I gave them over to their own stubborn heart, to walk in their own counsels."

Proverbs 6:24 "To keep you from the evil woman, from the flattering tongue of a seductress."

We clearly see in the scriptures presented how people, when led by their own lustful desires, can end up leaving the pathway of holiness and begin walking on the road of destruction. The question to ask yourself is how can people gain freedom from lust, which serves as the root of all sexual sin and stay free? What are some ways that church and ministry leaders can assist those on their team who struggle with lust?

A few practical examples for leaders include:

1. Pushing past personal fear in order to address and deal with the hard topics that affect the lives of those connected to you.

2. Set up a literature, pamphlet, or resource center in your church or ministry. Stock it with information on topics that actually affect people in real life.

3. Offer programs, workshops, and seminars to address issues faced by unmarried, widowed, or married adults.

When you take the time to deal with the stronghold of lust on the front end, it will enable you the opportunity to effectively dismantle and destroy the *smaller works* associated with it, which include adultery, fornication, masturbation, perversion, pornography, same sex attraction and other areas of sexual sin. These works are considered smaller because they can operate singularly, or cluster in groups, to defile the lives of those who have given the root of lust free access to dwell.

Overall, it is also important to note that once initial freedom has been obtained in any of these areas, experiencing and maintaining the benefit of the full deliverance falls into the hands of the individual person. Following, are some ways in which leaders can suggest to their team members who are struggling with sexual sin how they can stay free from the stronghold of lust and any of its smaller works.

1. Set aside time to read the Bible daily, meditating upon the healing promises of God.

2. Take time to stay connected and in fellowship with God on both a personal and corporate level. Connect with a church where the Bible is taught and not merely tolerated.

3. Change what is allowed access into their spirit. Be sensitive to what they watch on TV and view on the internet. Be more conscious of the different genres of music and books they listen to or read.

4. Increase their prayer life. A life of prayer is an essential component to maintaining deliverance.

5. If there are continued struggles, despite their best efforts, this reveals that addictive behavior is present. This is the point where you can direct them to seek the help of a trained

mental health professional who specializes in sexual addiction counseling and recovery.

Questions for Reflection

1. If someone on your church or ministry team has been openly acting out in a sexual manner towards others due to the negative effects of lustful thinking, how can you, as a leader, help redirect their focus? Explain.

2. Do you feel that there is a need for greater awareness and instruction in the church to help those who are dealing with the smaller works of lust such as adultery, pornography, masturbation, etc? Explain.

3. How did you assist any of your team members who dealt with the root of lust in the past? Do you feel that your methods were effective in helping them to gain freedom? Explain.

4. Have you personally experienced temptation in any area as it relates to the root of lust? If so, how were you able to gain freedom in this area? Explain.

Dissecting Adultery

Did you know:

Forty-one percent of married couples, whether one or both spouses, admit to adultery, either physical or emotional.

Fifty-seven percent of men admit to committing adultery in any relationship they have had.

Fifty-four percent of women admit to committing adultery in any relationship they have had.

Seventy-four percent of men say they would have an affair if they knew they would never be caught.

Sixty-eight percent of women say they would have an affair if they knew they would never be caught.[1]

In this chapter, several keys will be shared as we take a few moments to understand what the act of adultery is and how it operates.

Merriam Webster dictionary defines **adultery** as "voluntary sexual intercourse between a married man and someone other than his wife or between a married woman and someone other than her husband."

In II Samuel 11:2-5 we read about one of the most memorable stories in the Bible surrounding King David and Bathsheba. David was a man of honor and integrity, and was also known as a man after God's very heart. During a period of time, when David took his eyes off his divine assignment, the stronghold of lust was able to gain entry and his path was redirected because of his focus on the desires of his flesh.

---

[1] http://www.statisticbrain.com/infidelity-statistics

[2] Then it happened one evening that David arose from his bed and walked on the roof of the king's house. And from the roof he saw a woman bathing, and the woman was very beautiful to behold. [3] So David sent and inquired about the woman. And someone said, "Is this not Bathsheba, the daughter of Eliam, the wife of Uriah the Hittite?" [4] Then David sent messengers, and took her; and she came to him, and he lay with her, for she was cleansed from her impurity; and she returned to her house. [5] And the woman conceived; so she sent and told David, and said, "I am with child."

While David eventually repented for his sin of adultery with Uriah's wife, the consequences were far reaching, and eventually redirected the course of his divine assignment. However, despite this redirection, God always knew that David was a man after His own heart because whenever he was in error David always sought God to get back on track. David's hope was restored when God later blessed him and Uriah's wife with Solomon, his son of promise.

In recent years, the sexual sin of adultery has received much widespread attention through the media, in books, on the internet, in movies, and on TV. The very act of adultery, unfortunately, is no longer seen as the sin that the Bible speaks of. It is often portrayed as some sort of a badge of honor among those who often partake of its short-lived pleasures within our society. Men and women, alike, openly voice their approval of adultery as they try to justify why it is okay to share someone else's spouse. However, this is a lie and it teaches people that they are entitled to operate in a false covenant relationship outside of God's established order for marriages.

In years past, issues surrounding the subject of adultery were often kept hidden and rarely discussed openly. Many spouses suffered in silence as they dealt with the pressures and pain associated with the sexual indiscretion of their husbands or wives. Many were taught that if you did not talk about the adulterous act it would run its course and go away. Unfortunately, this was, and still is not the healthy way to work problems out within a marriage. The Father has shown couples a better way through His word. Before the fall of man He knew that the way of the flesh would be a serious issue in our time. The Bible shows us in black and white through David's story that there can be new life and love after an affair. God has already opened a way of escape for those who have yielded to the sexual sin of adultery. Know that if David embraced his deliverance and was able to get free from adultery by humbling himself before God, then those on your team who are in need of help can receive their freedom as well.

The time has come for the real truth about adultery to be exposed and challenged within our society. Men and women alike should know that it is not a badge of honor to be worn proudly. This type of misconception about marriage gives the offenders of a godly covenant a false sense of entitlement. Relationships established in adultery are not godly and can't be viewed in the same manner as couples who marry and connect together as one with God. True covenant marriage is an honorable institution designed by God so the marriage bed must remain undefiled.

When church and ministry leaders fall to the sin of adultery, it is important to direct them not to allow the condemnation of men or the enemy to prevent them from pursuing and embracing total freedom through Christ. Following are a few tips you can share with team members who are ready to walk in freedom from the sin of adultery. Let them know that it is time to:

1. Get up from where they have fallen and then repent to God.
2. Forgive and release themselves from the sin committed.
3. Set their house (life, family, and ministry) back in order.
4. Redirect their focus back to walking out their divine assignment.
5. Move forward in the healing process by helping others gain freedom from adultery.

Overall, it's important to reaffirm with your team members that God is a strong tower, deliverer, and restorer. He loves them just as He extended His hand of mercy to King David; He is now waiting to shower anyone who has been led astray with an overflow of His love and grace.

Questions for Reflection

1. What is your perception of adultery? Explain.

2. Have you directly or indirectly been affected by the negative effects of adultery? How did it make you feel? Explain.

2. Do you feel you are adequately prepared to counsel or minister to couples who are experiencing adultery within their marriage? Explain.

3. How would you respond if, even after extended counseling, a couple still decides to dissolve their marriage? Explain.

4. Do you see the sin of emotional or physical adultery as the means to end a covenant marriage? Why? Explain.

Print and Digital Pornography

Sex is the #1 subject that people search for on the Internet.

42.7% of Internet users view pornography.

Seventy percent of women keep their cyber activities secret.

Women, more than men, are likely to act out their behaviors in real life, such as having multiple partners, casual sex, or affairs. [2]

In this chapter, we will address the subject of print and digital pornography. Several solutions will be offered on how to help couples escape the negative and sometimes devastating impact that **pornography** can have upon covenant marriages.

Pornography is defined as:

1. The depiction of erotic behavior (as in pictures or writing) intended to cause sexual excitement.

2. Material (as books or a photograph) that depicts erotic behavior and is intended to cause sexual excitement

3. The depiction of acts in a sensational manner so as to arouse a quick intense emotional reaction (the *pornography* of violence).[3]

The increased speed of the Internet over the last decade has not only been beneficial for businesses, churches, ministries and schools, but it has also served as a widely accessible door for people to consistently view pornography. While the use of digital pornography is easy access for many, sales for print versions of magazines has been on the rise.

---

[2] http://internet-filterreview.toptenreviews.com/internet-pornography-statistics.html

[3] www.merriamwebster.com/dictionary/pornography

According to Family Safe Media data[4]:

Every second $3,075.64 is being spent on pornography.

Every second 28,258 Internet users are viewing pornography.

Every second 372 Internet users are typing adult search terms into search engines.

Every 39 minutes a new pornographic video is being created in the United States.

A good question to ask is why the subject of pornography is not only a touchy subject for people to talk about, but also why it is so hard for people to maintain freedom after being delivered from its clutches? What is it about pornography that people will neglect their spouses, families, ministries, and businesses in order to seek its pleasures? In order to help answer these questions and many more we will have to go back and look at the history of pornography.

The introduction of pornography for sexual arousal purposes debuted during the early 1800's. As times progressed and people became more relaxed about sexuality, new ways for them to increase their sexual arousal began to come into play. During this time in history, short films and printed pamphlets were introduced into the European market. It would be many years later before the first pornographic materials would begin to appear in the United States. [5]

In today's modern society, pornography can be seen via television, the internet, books, magazines, and in various forms of digital and audio media. At any time of day, you can turn on your television and before you can blink an eye, you can see pornographic images, often reserved for late night, openly expressed in daytime commercials, shows, and movie previews as well as on several cartoon networks.

The increase of social media sites has opened an even wider gateway by which people produce, and post, pornographic videos.

[4] http://familysafemedia.com/pornography_statistics.html#anchor12

[5] : http://www.livescience.com/8748-history-pornography-prudish-present.html

While there are many federal regulations and laws that govern and monitor the use and transmission of pornography, the influx of pornographic images and videos downloaded on social media sites show that these federal regulations are not as effective as they should be.

In an effort to combat this increasing social and spiritual ill, here are a few positive suggestions that you can utilize as an ongoing effort to help eradicate pornography from our midst.

1. Form a united front to address how pornography and other forms of sexual sin affect families and the church as a whole.

2. Set up discussion forums for teens, the unmarried and married couples about the negative effects pornography can have on their spiritual growth and walk with Christ.

3. Develop an open door policy where church and ministry team members can feel comfortable about talking with you or a designated church or ministry leader in confidence about areas where they may be struggling sexually.

4. Embrace those who have struggles with pornography in love. If possible, walk with them on their journey to freedom.

Following are a few passages of scripture that you can share with your team member to meditate on and to help serve as a reminder about the importance of walking in purity in every area of life. The Father wants us to be holy because He is holy. When we allow our lives to be consumed by things like pornography in order to please the flesh or satisfy the eyes, we show the Father that our desires are more important than His will for our lives.

Proverbs 4:23
"Keep your heart pure for out of it are the important things of life."

1 Peter 1:14-16
"As obedient children, do not conform to the evil desires you had when you lived in ignorance. But just as he who called you is holy,

so be holy in all you do; for it is written: "Be holy, because I am holy."

I Thessalonians 4:3
"God's will is for you to be holy, so stay away from all sexual sin.

Overall, in order for any person to stay free from any form of pornography, they must first accept accountability for their own actions by not transferring any blame to others. Also, they must come to terms with the negative effect that participating in the use of pornography has had on the operation of their marriage, family, ministry, or business. In the end, freedom from pornography is attainable when coupled with prayer, the word of God, and the support of others who can help hold them accountable.

Questions for Reflection

1. Have you personally viewed any print or digital pornography? Explain.

2. What went through your mind as you viewed these images? Explain.

3. Do you believe it is an easy task for people to gain freedom from pornography or any other sexual sin? Why? Explain

4. Why do you believe that you did not become addicted to pornography? Explain.

5. Do you feel that only certain people are prone to falling into sexual sin? Why? Explain.

When Leaders Fall

As leaders, it is important to have people on your team who are not only willing to stand in agreement with God's vision for your church or ministry, but who are also spiritually sensitive to remain in consistent prayer for you, especially when you are facing challenges.

In this chapter, we will discuss a few ways that church and ministry team members can learn how to stay focused while serving as spiritual agents of reconciliation when their leader, or those in direct authority, fall prey to adultery, pornography or any other sexual sin.

So, what happens when a trusted leader falls into sin? Who is there to help pick them up? Who will be there to sincerely minister and to help guide them back into the loving arms of the Father? As Christians, we are all directed to act in this role through the Word of God as stated in Galatians 6:1, which reads, "Brothers and sisters, if someone is caught in a sin, you who live by the Spirit should restore that person gently. But watch yourselves, or you also may be tempted."

So, how can you know if you have a faithful and committed team before any issues arise? One way to tell is by doing periodic assessments to see if there are people on your church or ministry team who often scatter when major issues come up and then later seek to re-gather when the blessings begin flowing. This is also an opportune time, as a leader, to listen to what is on the heart of those whom you directly cover and serve.

A good, solid team is comprised of a mix of people who are able to effectively communicate both verbally and nonverbally, with each other. They seek to look out for the needs of other team members in a non-controlling or unselfish manner. They understand the importance of working together in a spirit of excellence in order to achieve a common goal.

Having a faithful and good team by no means should serve as a license for you, as a leader, to habitually commit sin and then expect your team to stand idly by while you refuse to accept accountability and be responsible for your actions. However, the practical information presented here is to help assist your team as they seek to become the kind of team that can consistently walk in the type of love that encourages a leader to be the best that they can be through Christ. Ultimately, in order to maintain focus, the team must seek to keep God first in everything that they do.

Next, we will talk about the importance of restoration, and how to motivate team members to understand their roles as spiritual agents of reconciliation.

Why is Restoration so important?

1. Restoration is part of the reconciliation process initiated by the Father when He sacrificed His only Son Jesus in order reconcile people to Himself.

2. Fallen leaders are human and experience temptation to sexual sin just as those whom they lead. They should be afforded the same opportunity as other Christians to be restored and reconciled to the Father.

3. True restoration opens the door to a greater level of spiritual healing and growth.

Listed below are some suggestions to help motivate church and ministry teams to work towards restoring fallen leaders.

1. Seek out fresh new ways for your church or ministry to become established as a place of safety and refuge for leaders who may fall to sexual sin.

2. Instruct your team on how to become a non-judgment zone in order to guard against and prevent the spirit of shame from taking root in the lives of those who have fallen.

3. Be sincere in their attitude, approach, and response with others. Make sure team members seek to flow and stay in sync with one another.

4. Try not to force or rush the healing and deliverance process for anyone. Allow the Holy Spirit the opportunity to have

16

full control of the situation.

5. Instruct team members to respect and treat any fallen leader the same way that they would like to be treated if or when they experience their own spiritual/moral failure.

Lastly, every person experiences and goes through times of temptation. Although everyone may not experience the same temptation, each person has an area(s) that stand in need of spiritual cleansing. Romans 3:21-26 sums it up best, "[21]For all have sinned and fall short of the glory of God, [24]and all are justified freely by his grace through the redemption that came by Christ Jesus. [25]God presented Christ as a sacrifice of atonement, through the shedding of his blood to be received by faith. He did this to demonstrate his righteousness, because in his forbearance he had left the sins committed beforehand unpunished [26]he did it to demonstrate his righteousness at the present time, so as to be just and the one who justifies those who have faith in Jesus."

Questions for Reflection

1. Have you ever had a sin you were dealing with openly exposed? Explain.

2. How did the experience affect you and your walk with Christ? Explain.

3. What did you do to get back on track and in alignment with God? Explain.

4. Did what you experience open your eyes as to how easy it is for even leaders to fall into temptation? Explain.

5. What would you do differently if given another opportunity to escape the temptation? Explain.

Confidentiality and Disclosure

When it comes to the areas of confidentiality and disclosure, it is important for those who serve as church and ministry leaders to know and understand how to ethically operate within the proper boundaries.

Two important words to remember and adhere to as it relates to ministry and business are **confidentiality** and **disclosure**.

The word **confidentiality** comes from the word *confidential*, which means:
1. secret or private
2. entrusted with confidence
3. showing that you are saying something that is secret or private
4. trusted with secret or private information[6]

The word **disclosure** is defined as:
1. the act of making something known
2. something (such as information) that is made known or revealed [7]

When it comes to those who serve on your team, how do you rate them as it relates to understanding confidentiality and disclosure? Do you feel comfortable sharing with them or are you only able to share information with a select few? The word of God tells us in Proverbs 11:14 "Where there is no counsel, the people fall; But in the multitude of counselors there is safety."

If leaders cannot feel safe sharing important information as it relates to church or ministry business with members of their team this produces a breach in confidentiality. Leaders must feel secure with those who serve with them. As overseers of the church or ministry, everyone who serves under their leadership will also need to know that they too have a safe place to come when they are in need of advice or counsel.

What happens when the private covenant marriage issues of one

---

[6] www.merriamwebster.com/dictionary/confidential
[7] www.merriamwebster.com/dictionary/disclosure

of your team members becomes public knowledge? Regardless of who the person may be, anytime the private issues of an individual becomes public knowledge, immediately embarrassment, fear and shame enters. As spiritual agents of reconciliation one of our main goals is to serve as agents of hope and healing for others and not carriers of fear or shame.

As a leader, what do you say? How would you respond? First, you may want to ask yourself these two key questions:

(1) Should the issue be ignored and allowed the opportunity to run its course, *or*

(2) Should you, as the leader, intervene to offer your input and/or direction?

The course that you take as a leader can either help serve as a way to promote healing for all involved, or it can do quite the opposite and cause deep trust issues to surface within the relationships of those team members you are trying to help.

Following are three examples of releasing confidential information in a negative manner that leaders should seek to avoid.

1. Avoid approaching a team member with any information that they previously shared with someone else in confidence. This is considered third party information and is an unethical disclosure because the initial information was not personally shared with you.

2. Avoid releasing confidential information of absent team members even when masked as a prayer request. Always gain the team members permission first before sharing any type of private and confidential information.

3. Avoid being caught in the middle of conflicts where there has been a breach of confidentiality between team members. Always employ some type of conflict resolution strategy in order to foster peace. In the event these strategies prove unsuccessful, it may be wise to implement some type of confidentially and disclosure training for the whole team.

Now for three helpful and positive ways for assisting team

members as it relates to confidentiality and disclosure.

1. Empathize. Seek to recognize and understand the emotions of the team member involved. While a show of sympathy means to show care or concern for what they are experiencing, to empathize with them is like placing yourself in their shoes.

2. Check your approach and the manner in which you deal with or dispense sensitive, private information. In the event that you do decide to share (find it necessary to share) with staff or other leaders, ensure that they are trustworthy and have not had previous issues with maintaining confidentiality as it relates to sensitive matters. Overall, it is important for you to be prepared in advance to take ownership if any sensitive or confidential information is handled incorrectly.

3. Try going a step further by assisting with outside resources in order to bring forth a healthy resolution. When leaders show genuine concern to those on their team who are experiencing issues with sexual sin, even if not readily accepted, the assistance offered can one day help serve as a bridge to cross during the restoration process.

Following are several passages of scripture that focus on the subject of being trustworthy and a person of integrity.

Proverbs 11:13
A gossip betrays a confidence, but a trustworthy person keeps a secret.

Proverbs 12:22
The Lord detests lying lips, but he delights in people who are trustworthy.

Proverbs 13:17
A wicked messenger falls into trouble, but a trustworthy envoy brings healing.

Psalm 78:72
And David shepherded them with integrity of heart; with skillful hands he led them.

Hebrews 13:17
Have confidence in your leaders and submit to their authority, because they keep watch over you as those who must give an account.

Questions for Reflection

1. Do you consider your church or ministry to be a place of safety and refuge for those serving on your team? Explain.

2. Do you have established procedures in place to assist those within your church or ministry that may fall into adultery or other sexual sins? Explain.

3. If you or someone on your team falls to adultery or sexual sin, what would your initial response be? Why? Explain.

4. Have you ever experienced the mishandling of confidential information for one of your team members, and the manner in which it was disclosed greatly affected the creative/spiritual flow of the whole team? Explain.

5. Name some effective ways that you and your team members can safeguard your church or ministry from any issues surrounding the improper release of confidential information. Explain.

Final Words: Keys to Restoration

Prayerfully, the practical wisdom presented in this book will help to serve as a valuable resource for your church or ministry. It is important to note that initial deliverance and gaining full freedom from sexual sin may take longer for some to embrace than others. In the event that anyone on your team is faced with a difficult set of circumstances, know that it is okay to reach out to those who have been professionally trained in this area.

For those on your church or ministry team who have already made the decision to embrace their deliverance and walk free from all sexual sin, will also need ample time to go through the healing, restoration, and renewal process.

Whenever a person falls into any form of sin, they may experience short or long periods of guilt, sadness, and condemnation, ultimately leading to repentance and then ending in restoration. After a person has reached the point of repentance, this is where they have finally forsaken all pride in order to take accountability for the sin they have committed towards God. After a time of reflection, they will usually turn back to following God, which is when real restoration occurs.

For those who reject personal accountability for their actions, they will find that they will remain in a place of condemnation until there is a true change of heart.

Understand that restoring someone back to godly fellowship after a fall is not devaluing what they have done, however, it is biblical and it is important to restore people so they can see that all is not lost, and they can experience true liberty as God has purposed when He allowed His son to die for all sin.

Following are a few keys that you may use to help foster restoration for those on your team who may have recently experienced a setback in their walk with Christ.

1. Do not force the restoration process. Allow the Holy Spirit time to work. Above all things allow Him to be your guide because each individual deals with the restoration process differently.

2. Be on hand to assist your team member with additional prayer and counseling if necessary; however, don't allow yourself to become a spiritual crutch during the times when they should be embracing personal accountability.

3. If after several counseling sessions, your team member is experiencing difficulty in moving past this area of sexual sin, direct them to trained professionals who specialize in long-term sexual addiction recovery care.

4. Continue to pray and intercede for each team member, even after they have been restored. When led by the Holy Spirit, offer words of encouragement to let them know that you have not forgotten about them.

Following are a few scriptures, which highlight the importance of restoring others.

James 5:19-20 says, [19]My brothers and sisters, if one of you should wander from the truth and someone should bring that person back, [20]remember this: Whoever turns a sinner from the error of their way will save them from death and cover over a multitude of sins.

Galatians 6:1 reads. Brothers and sisters, if someone is caught in a sin, you who live by the Spirit should restore that person gently. But watch yourselves, or you also may be tempted.

Know that at any given moment, anyone can experience a lapse in spiritual judgment and yield themselves to the stronghold of lust thereby opening the door to other areas of sexual sin. When this happens, as children of the Sovereign God, it is important that we do not condemn people by cutting off their passageway to hope. But rather, extend God's love by helping to facilitate their deliverance and restoration back into God's divine will for their lives.

Prayer for Freedom from Shame

Heavenly Father, I enter into your presence to worship and honor you. I command my heart and mind to be at peace. I submit my body as a living sacrifice and stand in agreement with your divine will for my life.

I bring my team members who struggle with sexual sin before you and I thank you for the work you have already begun in them. I come against the spirit of shame and break its power over their lives.

I decree and declare that they will no longer walk in shame for the blood of Jesus has cleansed them of all sin. No longer will they live or operate under the curse of shame because they are now living in the freedom of Jesus Christ.

Father, I thank you for their new beginning and another opportunity to live, move, and have their total being submitted in love and reverence to you. In Jesus name, I pray. Amen

Prayer for Church and Ministry Leaders

Heavenly Father, I thank you for another opportunity to enter into your presence to worship you. Thank you for loving me despite my own shortcomings. Today, I ask that you forgive me for the times that I looked down upon and condemned those who had fallen to adultery or any form of sexual sin.

Forgive me for rejecting and not praying for those assigned to me in your love. Help me to become a safe place where people can come to find you and not a place where they are made to feel rejected or burdened down with fear and shame.

Help me to be a bright light in this dark world, not only for those who have fallen to sexual sin, but also for those who have fallen short in any area of life.

Heavenly Father, I thank you for not forsaking me during the times when I allowed my own sin to take my focus off of you. I desire to be more like Jesus so others can find hope and be fully restored back to you. Amen.

Sexual Addiction Treatment Resources

Affair Recovery Support Groups

After the Affair: Emotional Healing God's Way
Sessions for Individuals, Couples, and Groups
P. O. Box 754301
Memphis, Tennessee 38175
aftertheaffairseminars@yahoo.com

Affair Recovery
www.affairrecovery.com

Christian Recovery Programs

Darryl & Tracy Strawberry Christian Recovery Program
www.strawberryministries.org

Hope Quest Ministry Group
www.hqmg.org

Lifehouse Network
www.LighthouseNetwork.org

Church Crisis Response

RESTORE
www.restore.us

For Men Only

Free in Christ
www.befreeinchrist.com

For Women Only

Pure Intimacy
www.pureintimacy.org/h/help-for-female-sex-addicts

Pornography Support/Treatment Groups

Bethesda Workshops
www.BethesdaWorkshops.org

Blazing Grace
www.blazinggrace.org

LDS Hope and Recovery
www.ldshopeandrecovery.com

Porn Addiction Recovery
www.xxxchurch.com

Transparent Ministries
www.transparentministries.org/porn-stats

Sexual Addiction Support/Treatment Groups

L.I.F.E. Recovery International
www.freedomeveryday.org

Pure Life Alliance
www.purelifealliance.org

The Ranch
www.recoveryranch.com

Sex Addicts Anonymous
www.saa-recovery.org

Sex Help
www.sexhelp.com

Prayer of Salvation

If after reading this book you have a desire to know Jesus as your personal Lord and Savior, please take a few moments to pray the following prayer:

Heavenly Father,

I repent of all of my sins and right now I do confess that Jesus is the Son of God and that He died for the remission of my sins.

I believe that Jesus died and was buried and rose again, and is now seated at the right hand of God in Heaven.

I receive Him now as Lord of my life and I now commit to serve him for the rest of my days.

It's in Jesus' name I pray. Amen.

If you have just prayed this prayer and want more information about beginning your new life as a Christian, please write or email us at the following and we will be happy to send you a free booklet:

Unity Three Publications
PO BOX 754301
Memphis, TN 38175
arnitafields@yahoo.com

About the Author

Arnita LaFaye Fields is a wife, Christian counselor, and prophetic writer. She is the author of eleven books, which includes several collections of poetry. She is a co-author of three anthologies.

As a passionate advocate for emotionally healthy covenant marriages, she hosts a monthly online prayer and encouragement call for couples who are experiencing marriage difficulties.

Arnita was inspired to write the book series, *After the Affair: Emotional Healing God's Way* to help covenant couples, and ministry and marketplace leaders to emotionally heal after a physical or emotional affair.

As a prophetic writer, she pens words, blog posts, and articles that help edify, encourage, and instruct the Body of Christ on how to walk in the divine truth of the Heavenly Father.

In addition to being an award-winning author, Arnita is a graduate of Victory University with a Bachelors of Science degree in Psychology. She received an Associate of Arts degree in Psychology and Christian Counseling from Liberty University and earned a diploma in Biblical Counseling from Light University. She is currently completing graduate work at Regent University.

Arnita and her husband, Anthony, have been married 17 years and currently call Memphis, Tennessee home. If you would like to contact Arnita, you may send an email to arnitafields@yahoo.com or visit her blog at www.arnitalfields.blogspot.com

To order autographed copies (individual and/or bulk) of any of Arnita's books, or to arrange for Arnita to come and minister to your church, group, or special event, contact:
Arnitafields@yahoo.com

NOTES